MARK OESTREICHER

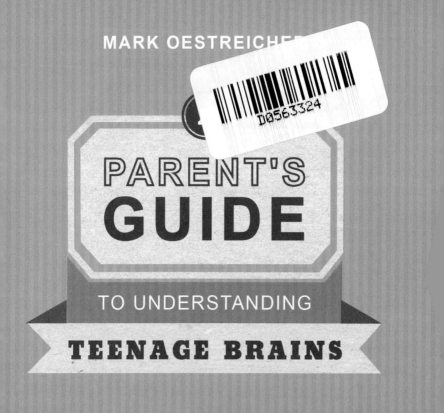

PARENT'S GUIDE

TO UNDERSTANDING

TEENAGE BRAINS

WHY THEY ACT THE WAY THEY DO

simply for parents

youthministry.com/TOGETHER

A Parent's Guide to Understanding Teenage Brains
Why They Act the Way They Do

© 2012 Mark Oestreicher

group.com
simplyyouthministry.com

Credits
Author: Mark Oestreicher
Executive Developer: Nadim Najm
Chief Creative Officer: Joani Schultz
Copy Editor: Rob Cunningham
Cover Art and Production: Veronica Preston

Scripture quotations taken from THE HOLY BIBLE, NEW INTERNATIONAL VERSION®, NIV® Copyright © 1973, 1978, 1984, 2011 by Biblica, Inc.™ Used by permission. All rights reserved worldwide.

ISBN 978-0-7644-8461-2

10 9 8 7 6 5 4 3 2   20 19 18 17 16 15 14 13

Printed in the United States of America.

CONTENTS

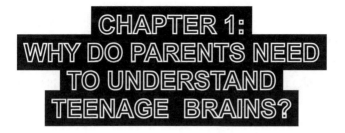

CHAPTER 1: WHY DO PARENTS NEED TO UNDERSTAND TEENAGE BRAINS?

The scene: Last week (as I write this), in the family room of my house, with nine sixth-grade boys. My youth ministry small group. I meet with them every Wednesday night for a combination of silliness and spiritual conversation.

Sixth-grade guys are normally fairly concrete in their thinking (we're going to talk a lot more about what that means in this book), and having spiritual conversations about abstract faith ideas is sometimes a bit of a challenge. So I was caught a bit off guard by Chris' amazing and semiconfrontational question: *Why won't anyone give me answers to my questions?*

He said it more as a statement, with a big dose of frustration and a hint of anger. And I couldn't have been more excited.

A few months back, our group had been talking about the incarnation (it was early December, and Christmas was on all of their minds). In the midst of my description of how amazing it is that God chose to insert himself *into* his own creation in order to connect with us, Chris interrupted. He sighed, and asked, "How do we know any of this is even true?"

At that moment, I wasn't sure if Chris really wanted an answer. Maybe I should have repeated Jesus' question to blind Bartimaeus: "What do you want me to do for you?" Or maybe a subtle variation: "What is it you're really asking, Chris?"

One of the other sixth-grade guys, clearly raised in church and loaded with preteen confidence, pushed back on Chris: "You shouldn't ask questions like that!"

I stepped in, affirming Chris strongly. I told him that asking questions like that is fantastic, and a super important part of following Jesus. I told him he should *never* feel awkward or ashamed or afraid to ask questions.

But I didn't answer his question. I saw it as an opportunity to affirm his asking, thinking that was the real issue.

It wasn't.

Now, these months later, Chris was upset and had obviously been wrestling with this question and others like it for a long time. He went on to say that he'd asked more than one person, and everyone kept telling him it was good to ask—but no one would answer his questions. He even pointed to a book I'd written for middle schoolers about faith (which I'd given to him), and stated that the book did the same thing!

Yup, it was absolutely time to answer Chris' questions. I set aside my plans, and asked him what he wanted to know. He led with: "Well, I want to know how we know the Bible is true."

Another guy jumped in, asking, "What if we get to heaven and find out we had *the wrong* God?"

So I dived in. I affirmed, over and over again, how important it was to wrestle with these things, and how it's a part of them growing into men of faith. I couched my responses with, "This is what I believe to be true, and why I'm confident in my explanation; but you might need more than my answers, and that's where faith comes in."

Here's what I absolutely knew in that moment: Chris was—rather gloriously, I will say—revealing the interaction of adolescent brain development and faith. Chris was showing me his changing brain.

And without an understanding of teenage brain development, I might have either missed the moment or shut down his curiosity with easy answers that didn't satisfy the intensity of the questions.

I am both passionate about and fascinated by teenage brains. As a 30-year youth ministry veteran and a father of two teenagers, I find that my continually growing understanding of teenage brains informs almost everything I do in ministry and parenting.

My hope is that this little book will give you some insight, some "oh, that explains things" moments. But my bigger hope is that, as a result of these insights, you will be more engaged in the life of the teenager in your home. If I could separate parents of teenagers into two broad categories, based on years and years of observing thousands of parent/teen relationships, I would use these categories:

- Homes where at least one parent is meaningfully engaged in the life of the teenager.

- Homes where parents are physically present, but not meaningfully engaged in the life of the teenager.

As a parent of two wonderful but not angelic teenagers, I know firsthand how challenging that first bullet is. My own two teenagers often give me the impression that they don't really want me involved in their lives (that's a smoke screen, by the way, and part of teenagers' developmental need to differentiate themselves from us as parents). They seem to want more independence than I would have assumed they were ready for. They (Liesl and Max are their names, and I'll be telling stories about them throughout this book) frustrate my attempts at staying engaged, and regularly push my buttons.

Add to that: We live in a culture where the ideas of what it means to be a good parent have shifted dramatically. We're constantly told to treat our teenagers like children, that they're not ready to be responsible (not capable, even). We're told that we're irresponsible parents if we allow our children to take hold of meaningful responsibility or to experience the consequences of poor choices.

Bottom line: Parenting teenagers is *really difficult*!

There are a host of variables involved in great parenting. We can't address all of them in the scope of this pocket-sized book. But I promise, the glimpse you'll gain into the development and function of your teenager's brain will help you!

The Biggest Change in Teenagers

Of course, you know your son or daughter is changing. After all, we know that the teenage years are years of transformation from childhood to adulthood. They're like a strange river crossing, where children set off from one bank in a dinghy of innocence and confidence, and—after an often choppy and close-to-capsizing fording—step onto the opposite bank resembling something close to an adult.

But most parents focus on the externals: physical growth, body change, sexual development, voice changes. That's the obvious stuff, and it's happening right before our eyes. My 14-year-old son recently returned from a two-week class trip, and my wife and I simultaneously said, when he was walking toward us at the airport, "He looks older!"

Those physical changes are a big deal, and I wouldn't minimize them for a second. Those changes are visible to everyone, but they're *mostly* visible to the teenager experiencing them. They live with their physical changes every day and see their whole bodies in a way no one else does. Teenagers have a tormented combination of hope and fear when it comes to their physical development. They've been told, nonstop, what their bodies are *supposed* to look like, and they live on a razor-sharp continuum of "My body's not right" and "Things are starting to change."

In fact, my contention has always been that you can't find a single teenager, anywhere, who doesn't think at some point (often for extended periods of time—even years) that they're *turning out wrong*. They think they're too short or too tall, too thin or too fat, too behind the developmental curve or too ahead of it. They want the developmental bits they haven't yet achieved, and are often awkward and uncomfortable with those same developmental bits once they've got them.

Yeah, the physical changes are a really big deal. And we could write books about that (in fact, some of this is covered in three of the other books in this series: *A Parent's Guide to Understanding Teenage Guys*, *A Parent's Guide to Understanding Teenage Girls*, and *A Parent's Guide to Understanding Sex and Dating*). But I do not believe that the physical changes are the most important changes of adolescence.

I believe the most significant change in teenagers is what takes place in their brains. That might seem a little crazy to you, but let me explain myself. The brain change (which is, if we want to get technical, also a physical change) reorients every aspect of life for teenagers, preparing them for adulthood.

Looking at cognitive change by itself is a big enough deal (we'll cover this extensively in the following pages). But the reason I believe that brain change is the biggest change in teenagers is because it's the linchpin for all the other changes that shape the teenage experience, including emotional change, relational change, independence, and spiritual change.

And there's no question about it, the changes in your teenager's brain are the primary source for conflict with parents. You won't often experience tension with your teen about their growth in height! But no doubt you will experience plenty of friction in areas like conflicting expectations, rules, responsibilities, emotional outbursts, self-expression, media choices, clothing and style choices, friend selection, boundaries, priorities, and a host of other issues that are *directly* tied to brain development.

Yup, it's time to get to know your teenager's brain.

Teenage Brains Are Not the Same as Yours

Don't worry; I'm never going to get too technical in this book. There are three reasons for that:

1. There's not space in a 12,000-word book for much detail.

2. You would likely not be very interested in the technical, medical details.

3. I'm not the guy to write that kind of book. I'm a practitioner, both as a youth worker and a parent. (Remember that old TV commercial where the actor said, "I'm not a doctor, but I play one on TV," as if that was supposed to help us trust his medical input? Maybe I should say, "I'm not a neurologist, but I pretend to be one in youth ministry.")

I have, however, read a bunch on this subject. And I've had long conversations with brain docs. I've digested and reflected, looked at brain scans, and watched for years how the things I was learning about teenage brains did or didn't line up with what I was reading.

And more than anything else there is to know about teenage brains, there's this: Their brains are not yet adult brains.

It's interesting, though, that this is a mixed bag of limitations and opportunities. For example, teenage brains are still significantly underdeveloped in a couple of critical areas (we'll talk about this in Chapter 5), which adds great challenge to a teenager's ability to exercise wisdom, make reasoned choices, control impulses, and interpret emotions.

But while teenagers have certain limitations, due to their still-developing brains, they also possess a host of abilities we adults are slowly losing. It's funny to me (I'll have to ask God about this at some heavenly moment) that while teenagers have natural limits on decision-making and other important brain functions, they are at the peak of brain function in a bunch of areas I wish (as a 49-year-old) I was stronger in! For example, pattern recognition, brain speed, and memory of details all grow exponentially during the young and middle teen years, peaking between (depending on the exact function) 16 and 22 years old.

Some researchers have recently begun suggesting that the "limitations" of the teenage brain are actually benefits. The suggestion, in a nutshell, is that you and I are stodgy.

I mean, no researcher says that, of course. But they're saying that teenagers' natural risk-taking behavior and lack of inhibitions and "good" decision-making is what allows them to discover the boundaries in the world. They're able to step over the line in a way we normally wouldn't, which helps them discover where the line actually exists.

This isn't just about moral issues or classic risk-taking behaviors such as drinking, drugs, and sex. Let's consider a neutral case study:

Devin is a 15-year-old guy who isn't overly outgoing, but he has a few good friends. He's not a particularly popular kid, but has been genuinely content with the small constellation of peers who he hangs out with. Along comes an opportunity, strange as it seems to Devin, to hang out with an edgy mixed-gender group of teenagers who Devin perceives to *have* something (coolness, swagger, maturity, whatever) that he wants but doesn't possess. The problem becomes clear, however, that for Devin to associate with this new group of potential friends, he'll be forced to leave his old friends behind. Devin takes the risk without a second thought, turning his back on his old friends. And when the new friendship group doesn't turn out to be what he'd hoped it would, Devin is left friendless for a period of time.

But while this experience might be a horrible experience for Devin, it was a fantastic learning experience. Devin has learned (we hope he learned—at least he had the opportunity to learn) boatloads of information about loyalty, relational risk, perceived coolness, and betrayal. You and I would likely not have taken the risk, which would have been the better choice in this case, but we have already learned those lessons.

I see the creativity of God all over this, by the way. I know that while I can learn and grow in lots of ways, the most significant learning and growth in my life usually comes from situations that involved risk and failure (even at my ripe middle-age). But I'm less prone to risk (and therefore, failure) than I was when I was in my teenage years, which naturally means I'm learning less. Do you see the connection? How cool that God dreamed up teenage brains to be naturally risk-taking!

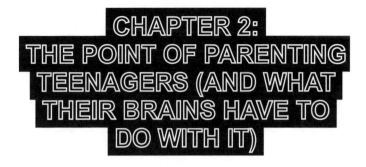

CHAPTER 2:
THE POINT OF PARENTING TEENAGERS (AND WHAT THEIR BRAINS HAVE TO DO WITH IT)

With her permission, I'd like to tell you a bit about my daughter, Liesl. This feels a bit vulnerable to me (because I like my daughter, and I fear—if I'm honest—that you might judge her or me). But I think it might prove helpful.

Liesl is 18 as I write this and will graduate from high school in less than two weeks. She's been accepted into the University of Redlands but has deferred for a year so she and a friend can volunteer for nine months in England, Scotland, and India. As you might imagine, I'm a little nervous about my 18-year-old daughter spending nine months without adult supervision in Europe and India, but I am also *so* proud of her and think this will be an indescribably powerful growing-up experience.

She's a unique one. Liesl has dreadlocks. Her only birthday wish when turning 18: a tattoo. She has a few more piercings than I would prefer, including some in her ears that we have battled over, due to their size (of the holes, that is, not the earrings). She has what could only be described as a very unique clothing style, consisting mostly of secondhand and personally modified clothes and a stuffed sheep backpack she carries with her everywhere (it even has its own Facebook® page). She plays the bass guitar (which works for her interest in 1970s and 1980s punk music), keyboards (which she played in the high school worship band at our church), and viola (which she leveraged to get a small music scholarship for college). She took over an environmental group at our church, providing leadership that had previously been filled by an adult. She made a film for her senior project, and was voted prom queen. She still likes to be around us and her younger brother (a miracle right there!) but is extremely independent and strong-willed. Oh, and she has a pet snake—an albino milk snake named Amii who eats a mouse per week.

Liesl also has been sent home from school more than once, has caused us a few sleepless nights, has lied to us, was arrested once, and has one of the messiest rooms I can imagine (it's terrifying to me at times, and hard not to make it a "hill to die on"). And wow, have we struggled (translation: fought) over homework.

Liesl is fairly happy. And I'm glad about that. But our primary parenting goal was never that she would be happy.

Liesl is fairly ambitious and resilient, which are great traits that will serve her well in life. But "success" born of ambition and resiliency has never been our primary parenting goal.

Clearly, as you can tell from my description of her, Liesl is creative and unique. I love that about her. But it was never our primary parenting objective that she turn out creative and unique.

Liesl is, for the most part, very nice to people of all sorts. I'm thrilled about this character trait, but—are you starting to see the pattern here?—our primary goal has never been that she would be "nice."

Our primary parenting goal, particularly through her sometimes-turbulent teenage years, has been that she would become an adult. She *has* become an adult (an aspiring adult, maybe, or an apprentice adult), and I could not be more proud.

She really is ready to launch. I'm sure she has plenty of missteps, blunders, bad choices, and unfortunate consequences yet to experience. But she's ready to be an adult, and my job as a parent is mostly complete. She will *not* be an extended adolescent who hangs around our home for another 10 years, because she is responsible and possesses a wonderful combination of autonomy and the ability to ask for help.

Why did I use this printed real estate to tell you about my daughter? Because for all her imperfections and mine, focusing on the right parenting goals is one thing, thank God, I think my wife and I did right.

The goal of parenting a teenager should not be creating miniature versions of ourselves. It shouldn't be making nice, compliant citizens. And it sure shouldn't be raising "successful" wage earners.

The primary goal of parenting a teenager is to raise an adult. By the time your son or daughter finishes high school (and I hope you'll see this in fits and starts before that point), he or she should be able to say with confidence, "I'm ready to take responsibility for myself, for my decisions— good and bad—and for my influence in the world."

Now, you won't be surprised when I tell you that has everything to do with brain development, right? Healthy adults (or post-teenagers who are launching into adulthood) have God-given and God-designed brains that assist them well in the primary marker of adulthood: responsibility.

Extended Adolescence and Parenting Brains

In the last 10 years, adolescence has extended so quickly, it's almost impossible to pin it down for description. With puberty starting at younger and younger ages (10 ½ or 11 is the average for girls these days), the entry point into adolescence has dropped. Of course, culture (and media, particularly) has added to this drop. But the upper end of adolescence has shifted even more dramatically.

Even 20 years ago, the upper end of adolescence was firmly planted at the combination of turning 18 and graduating from high school (this, by the way, was already an extension from the cultural norm earlier in the 1900s, which had adolescence ending at 16 years old). And the "normal distribution" (the bell curve that describes the 80 percent who would be described as "normal") was very narrow. Once you hit 18 and graduated, the cultural expectation was that you would start to take responsibility for yourself and function as an adult. All kinds of laws, freedoms, and expectations came around that age to calcify it (for a time): the right to vote, the age one can join the military, the right to represent oneself in court or sign a legal document, the responsibility for one's own medical care, the right to get married without parental permission, and the legal drinking age (for many years; though, this has been raised to 21 in all states).

But massive shifts in culture at large, parenting, economics, and other forces have extended adolescence well beyond the teen years. Dr. Robert Epstein, a noted psychologist and former editor of Psychology Today, wrote a radical book a few years ago called *Teen 2.0*. In the book, Epstein writes:

"…Until about a century ago… adolescence as we know it barely existed. Through most of human history, young people were integrated into adult society early on, but beginning in the late 1800s, new laws and cultural practices began to isolate teens from adults, imposing on them an increasingly large set of restrictions and artificially extending childhood well past puberty. New research suggests that teens today are subjected to more than ten times as many restrictions as are most adults, and adulthood is delayed until well into the twenties or thirties.

It's likely that the turmoil we see among teens is an unintended result of the artificial extension of childhood."[1]

Hold on to your seat for this next bit: Adolescent specialists now say that adolescence, on average, extends to 30 years old. In fact, adolescence is so long now (almost 20 years—a full ¼ of the human lifespan!) that it's talked about in three stages:

- Young teen (11-14)

- Late teen (15-20)

- Emerging adult (20-30) (By the way, this stage was originally called "late adolescence." But no 20-something wants to be called an adolescent, so "emerging adult" is the new politically correct terminology.)

Of course, the normal distribution (that bell curve of normalness) has flattened without the cultural agreement we had around 18 years old. So today we have 21-year-olds who are fully functioning as responsible adults, and 35-year-olds who are still stuck in a cycle of extended adolescence.

When I talk about this shift with parents, they usually respond that the primary reason must be economic— that it's more difficult for a young adult to be financially independent than it was even a decade or two ago. Certainly this is a factor, but I don't think it's the biggest factor (nor do those who study this). Parents also suggest that the "need" for more young adults to pursue college and graduate education explains this shift. Again, this is a factor, but I believe it's as much a result as it is a cause.

Really, this shift is easier to understand than it might first appear. Think of it this way: If the definition of adulthood is "owning responsibility for one's self," then wouldn't it make sense that the giving of responsibility is the thing that's missing? It's not (primarily) the fault of young adults and teenagers that they don't "take" responsibility. Responsibility is more often given than taken. The major shift, then, has been that we no longer provide responsibility (and the expectation that goes along with it) to teenagers and young adults. And in our misguided ideas about *protecting* our children, we often remove the consequences to their choices, which completely undermines the learning about responsibility that consequences provide.

Here's how this connects to our topic of teenage brains: Responsibility and decision-making are functions of the frontal lobes (more on that in Chapter 5). And while that part of the brain isn't fully developed until around 25 years old, the brain has an amazing ability to compensate for weaknesses. Think of it this way:

responsibility given ➡ **responsibility experienced** ➡ **responsibility learned**

Sure, there's a *will* aspect to this, but responsibility is first and foremost a function of the brain. And a teenager who is never given *meaningful* responsibility (*meaningful* is a key word there) can't be expected to *be* responsible.

As a quick aside before we move on, the other major factor contributing to extended adolescence is the isolation of teenagers (and young adults). Teenagers spend almost every waking minute in a homogeneous grouping of peers (or alone). Today's teenagers have almost no opportunity to spend time with adults *in the world of adults* (the only time they spend with adults is when the adults come into the world of teenagers). As a result, teenagers and young adults have little opportunity to practice being what I like to call *apprentice adults*.

When teenagers spend time with adults in the world of adults, their brains are shaped, as neural pathways that serve responsibility and other adult functions are strengthened. If you woke up one day with a third arm (other than the clothing challenges, a third arm would be handy at times!) that had never been used—it was fresh-out-of-the-box—you wouldn't expect it to have any strength or usefulness until you exercised it a bit. The same is true of teenage brains and responsibility. They have the capacity, but it has to be exercised!

Engagement Over Control

There's been a significant shift in parenting styles over the last decade or two. I find it rather troubling. And what I find particularly interesting is that when I'm asked to lead conversations and seminars for parents of teenagers, and I talk about this destructive shift, parents agree with me. Yet I'm quite sure that most of them fall into the broad cultural pressure to parent in this "new" style. In other words: It's difficult to parent in a way that's different from everyone around you!

The new style: control.

Maybe it's due to the fear so many parents live with, a fear that our world is changing so quickly, and much of those changes have inherent in them at least some perception of threat. I was reading Pulitzer Prize-winning author Michael Chabon's recent nonfiction book *Manhood for Amateurs* and found striking a section where he wrote about teaching his daughter to ride her bike. Chabon writes:

"Recently, my younger daughter, after the usual struggle and exhilaration, learned to ride her bicycle. Her joy at her achievement was rapidly followed by a creeping sense of puzzlement and disappointment as it became clear to both of us that were was nowhere for her to ride it—nowhere I was willing to let her go. … Soon after she learned to ride, we went out together after dinner, she on her bike, with me following along at a safe distance behind. What struck me at once on that lovely summer evening, as we wandered the streets of our lovely residential neighborhood at that after-dinner hour that had once represented the peak moment, the magic hour of my own childhood, was that we didn't encounter a single other child." [2]

I have no interest in trying to idealize the past. In truth, parenting styles throughout history have each had their own inherent blind spots. But this control thing is fairly new. And it has landed on us with juggernaut speed and force.

I don't question the *motivation* of parents who spend so much effort attempting to control every aspect of their children and their children's experience of the world. I start with the assumption that their motivation is honorable and good. But the obsessive approach to control is squeezing the life out of children and teenagers, *and* harming them by dramatically limiting the very interactions with the world that should be shaping their brains through the occasionally brutal but usually instructive process of trial and error.

Maybe this is a slight overstatement, but safety has become the trump card of parenting. Parents are considered "good" if they protect their children.

Now, I'm all for boundaries (as you'll see in the next section). But I want teenagers (including the two living in my house) to have a rich diet of experiences and challenges and obstacles and scrapes and "should I or shouldn't I?" moments that will prepare them for adulthood!

I was sitting with Dr. Robert Epstein (the author of *Teen 2.0* I mentioned earlier), chatting about extended adolescence and parenting. I asked him how these ideas were shaping his own approach to parenting. He responded by saying he was trying to shift from parenting by control, to parenting by facilitation, where facilitation means "identifying and nurturing competencies." Wow, what a different mindset. What a healthy mindset. What a great way to play an active and helpful role in shaping the brains of our teenage children, preparing them for adulthood.

Parenting by control is not relational. It's mechanistic. And it doesn't, ultimately, provide you *or* your teenage son or daughter with the relationship you both desire (yes, your son or daughter *does* desire a relationship with you, even if all indications might be to the contrary).

This is why I'm convinced that one of the most important values we can have as parents of teenagers is to stay engaged in their lives (and they in ours). If you forfeit engagement in an attempt to control certain desirable outcomes, you've squandered both your influence and your relationship.

Engagement isn't easy. It takes intentionality and time and compromise and flexibility and apologies and a willingness to be awkward.

At the end of the day, you might be able to control some aspects of your teenager's life and behavior, and thus control some aspects of shaping his or her brain; but it's a dead end that doesn't deliver on its promise. Once you lose the relationship, you hand your child's brain over to every other shaping force in our world.

But engagement delivers, because it consistently puts you both in moments of triumph and in moments of pain and failure, alongside your teenager. And when you're living alongside teenagers, you get the opportunity to be a brain-shaper with adulthood in mind.

Boundaries and Freedom

In order to grow in "processing strength," teenage brains desperately need the opportunity to explore, risk, test hypotheses, and experience failure. So some amount of meaningful freedom is essential. Even young teenagers need to begin experiencing a certain amount of freedom as they move into the early stages of abstract thinking and exploring both how the world works and their place in it.

But freedom without any boundaries at all is overwhelming and damaging to the development of teenagers.

My wife is finishing a graduate degree in somatic psychology, a branch of psychology that focuses on trauma and its resolve, with an understanding that trauma often resides in our bodies.

One of the metaphors I have learned from my wife is how a wild animal responds to threat. The healthiest response from an animal, when an unexpected item or action occurs in its space, is orienting to the new item. But when a wild animal is threatened, it has three possible responses:

- Flight. In this state, the animal, assuming the threat is more powerful, high-tails it.

- Fight. This one's pretty obvious, right?

- Freeze. When there's confusion on the part of the animal, as to whether it should run away or fight, it can get stuck in this state. This is the "deer in the headlights," and is often a source of trauma.

I offer that metaphor because I think it explains why both freedom and boundaries are so important for teenagers. They need to be given the space to explore their world, but too much freedom can easily move teenagers into either horrible choices with enormous lifelong implications (this part is more obvious), or a freeze state of not being sure how to proceed.

I have seen this hundreds, maybe thousands of times in teenagers. Parents who control their teenager's experience don't allow for the learning that comes from exploration (which should naturally lead to the learning that comes from orienting, flight, or fight). But parents who provide no boundaries at all (or boundaries that are way too wide, developmentally) can damage their kids' growth—including the critical growth of their brain functions—by putting them in a place of being overwhelmed (freeze).

That might all make great sense to you, but you might be left with the question, "So, how do I know where to set the boundaries?" Good question!

Unfortunately, there's not a formula for this (which is one of the reasons why staying engaged in your teenager's life is so deeply critical, so you can make adjustments in response to what you're observing and hearing). As a general rule, the process of parenting a teenager is all about *expanding* the boundaries as you observe that your son or daughter has become comfortable and reasonably responsible with the amount of freedom you've previously given them.

As an example: My wife and I had to figure out a workable solution for what music Liesl (and now Max) was allowed to listen to or own at various points during the teenage years. Music choice is a great area to give some freedom to your teenagers, because it's a creative form of self-expression. You don't want to require that they only listen to what you like, right? So when she was in middle school, we created a boundary that Liesl could choose the music on her iPod®, including the purchasing of some music, but that I had to approve them all. I spent more time than I would have preferred looking up lyrics online. My basic guideline, which I'd communicated to Liesl, was that we didn't want her listening to music with a bunch of bad language, or music that spoke poorly of women, or that was destructive in some other way. But within those guidelines, she had a developmentally appropriate amount of freedom, including listening to music that we didn't "like."

When Liesl proved fairly responsible with that amount of freedom, around 14 years old, we expanded the boundaries a bit. This expansion had less to do with what we preferred (we still didn't want her listening to music that crossed those previous lines) and more to do with the "approval process." I no longer checked the lyrics of all the songs on an album, and she only had to tell me the name of the band. If I wasn't familiar with the musician or band, I would do a little research, with the commitment to get back to her within 24 hours. And by time she was 17, we told her she could make her own music choices but asked that she be respectful to her younger brother's presence and her influence on him.

We used the same process of expanding the boundaries when it came to social media. Liesl and Max were each allowed to have a Facebook account when they turned 13 (the age at which Facebook allows user accounts without lying). They both wanted a Facebook page prior to 13, but we held our ground, even allowing them to get a Gmail address for early forays into online communication. But the rule with all their online presences was that I was to always have the password and would regularly log on to their accounts to observe what they'd been up to. And while younger, both kids were expected to only access social media stuff (including email) when they were in a public space of our house. When Liesl had some mildly objectionable material on her Facebook page (or, back in the day, on her MySpace® page!), I would speak to her about it, ask for a correction, but only tighten the boundaries if the behavior repeated. In other words, she was allowed to make mistakes.

Once Liesl had proved fairly responsible with her online freedoms (and in other areas of life), I significantly diminished the level of accountability. Now that she's 18, I wouldn't think of telling her she can't be on Facebook in her bedroom, or requiring her to delete a distasteful post from one of her friends. I might still point it out, but her current freedoms wouldn't cause me to require a change. She might still cross the line, but she has to learn the consequences of that on her own.

That's the art of parenting teenagers—creating clear and ever-expanding boundaries, within which teenagers can exercise a real but developmentally appropriate level of freedom. That's brain-training, baby!

My youth ministry passion and experience has mostly been with middle schoolers. I dig 'em, which I realize puts me in a small minority of humans. One of the greatest things I love about middle schoolers is how they constantly teeter-totter back-and-forth between concrete thinking and abstract thinking.

Here's an example: I was teaching Sunday school on the subject of courage, and decided to do something a bit strange. I had already planned on teaching the group how the word *courage* means, in its etymology, "to have a full heart" (*cour* means "heart" in Latin). I was going to explain that we can't fill our own hearts, that we need God to do that for us. But I got a bit weird. I put on a fake cooking show, using sheep hearts I'd picked up from a butcher, while explaining how we can have more courage.

I brought out the sheep hearts, cut the tops off of them, and then spent some time talking about the ingredients that go into having a full heart.

- I broke a couple of eggs (using them as a simple illustration for the Trinity) and separated the whites into a bowl, explaining how we can never have a full heart unless the Holy Spirit gives us strength.

- I added breadcrumbs to the bowl, saying they represented our willingness to respond to God.

- Then I added cayenne pepper and some other spice, saying they represented a positive attitude.

As I stirred the mixture with my hands, I explained how having only two of those ingredients won't cut it:

- With only our willingness and positive attitude, but no Holy Spirit, the whole thing falls apart.

- With the Holy Spirit and our willingness, but a bad attitude, the mixture is flavorless.

- With the Holy Spirit and a positive attitude, but no willingness, there's no substance and nothing happens.

Then I stuffed the mixture into one of the sheep hearts and talked about how having courage isn't the same thing as having no fear. We can be scared but still move out with courage. As I cleaned up my hands, I talked about David running at Goliath, and guessed that he might have been thinking something like: "I'm about to pee myself right now because I'm so scared—but I have courage because God gave it to me, and I'm not going to back down, you freak!"

I'll admit, I was pretty proud of myself. It had taken a little extra prep work, but I'd given the middle schoolers a lesson that had a magical combination of insightful truth *and* something that held their attention and would not quickly be forgotten. (I hope you know I'm mocking myself here. Read on.)

These are the kinds of responses I heard later that morning and week:

- "Did you actually eat that?"

- "I hate cayenne pepper."

- "That was animal cruelty."

Those who were at least attempting to connect my cooking show illustration to the spiritual truth said things like:

- "Wait, so did David cut out Goliath's heart and eat it after he killed him?"

- "So, we're supposed to be like, um, spicy Christians?"

- "Would the *rest of God* have ruined it, if it hadn't only been the egg white part?"

To be fair, I did have a few kids (eighth-graders, a bit older than some of the other commenters), who seemed to get it and find it memorable. They might not have remembered the recipe, but I think many of them got the "Courage requires a full heart, and only God can fill your heart" main point.

The reason so many of the middle schoolers didn't "get it" wasn't just because it was a weird and distracting illustration (though that may have been true also). The reason so many of them didn't follow was because my beautiful culinary illustration was wildly abstract, and middle schoolers are notoriously weak when it comes to abstract thinking.

If your kid had a puberty party when he or she launched, physically, into the teen years, God would show up with a beautifully wrapped gift. Inside: abstract thinking. Really, the onset of abstract thinking, which starts at puberty, is a wonderful, glorious jetpack of seeing the world in a new way. Abstract thinking changes *everything*.

Children and preteens do not have the cognitive ability to think abstractly. And teenagers shift in and out of it constantly on their long march to conquer it and make it useful. In the meantime, throughout the teenage years, kids are thinking concretely one moment and dabbling in abstraction the next. You might rightly assume that young teenagers will more often be in concrete-land, and that older teenagers should have a decent working use of abstraction, but it's not that simple, unfortunately.

Abstract thinking, in a nutshell, is thinking about thinking. And it has gigantic implications for the daily life of your teenager and your life as a parent.

Big Implication #1: Speculation

The onset of abstract thinking has a bunch of perspective-altering implications, but there's no question that one of the biggest is the new ability to truly speculate. Children and preteens don't really have the cognitive ability to speculate—to run "what if" and "why might that be" scenarios in their minds.

This speculation ability is so everyday to us as adults that it's a bit difficult to imagine life without it. When you consider a choice, like a job change, you immediately begin the process of running through potential possibilities in your mind:

- What might the new job be like?

- What might the culture at the worksite feel like?

- What might be some of the impact on my life and family?

- What's the risk involved?

- How would I feel if I *don't* put my hat in the ring for this job?

Children can only draw more singular, concrete observations about what might happen ("It will be good" or "It will be bad").

We exercise our speculation abilities not only on major life choices (like a job change), but also constantly on minor choices. I'm writing in a hotel room at this moment, in between youth ministry training events, and I just made the simple decision about the point at which I would pause writing and go down to the lobby for the free breakfast. An inconsequential decision, in many ways, but I still, naturally and intuitively, made that minor choice with a cloud of "go now" and "go later" scenarios in my mind.

You've likely experienced exasperation at some point with your teenager, when you just couldn't understand why he or she didn't think through the obvious (to you) implications of a particular choice. "Didn't you think it would impact your grade if you didn't turn in your homework?" "Why would you think it was OK to light those firecrackers in the school parking lot?"

Teenagers possess the ability to speculate, but they're not very good at it. It's like a brand-new muscle that's just been added to their repertoire of thinking abilities—but it's a weak, flabby muscle that's never been used. Speculation takes practice and requires regular use before it's dependable and immediately available without intentionality.

But it's there, and it works. And even without intentionality, speculation starts to creep into the thought processes of young teenagers, and it's a regular visitor for middle and older teenagers. Think of it this way: When children go through that wonderful and annoying phase of life where they ask "why?" incessantly, they're merely looking for a simple causal relationship. But when teenagers ask "why?" (which, by the way, is often not verbalized), they're seeking a broader understanding—a metaphysical understanding, really—of the complexities of life.

I remember a specific time, a couple of years ago, when my son Max was about 12 years old. Max was a particularly black-and-white thinker; combined with a strong sense of justice, he always saw things as right or wrong. Some students in his class got in trouble for some behaviors that were mildly sexual in nature, but crossed the line of what Max (and his teacher!) believed to be "right." I remember talking with him about it, and how much it bothered him. I asked him about what he was feeling. He was clearly feeling *something* very strongly—that was obvious on his face and in his body language. But he couldn't put words to it. After a very long pause and a sigh or two, he said something like, "I don't know how to describe it, but I don't like it."

Max wouldn't have been so internally conflicted two years earlier; the situation would have merely been "wrong." But now it was more complex. It bothered him, but he couldn't quite pin it down.

The beautiful, and occasionally harrowing, aspect of this new speculation ability is that it opens up a world of potential and opportunity for teenagers. In a way, that might feel threatening to you—teenagers start questioning your values and choices, because they're starting to see that other values and choices were or are available. They often start asking tough questions about faith (more on that in Chapter 4), or swapping out their hobbies or style for a new bit of exploration, or shifting friendships (based on the speculative assumption that new friends will provide more of what they think they're looking for in a friendship).

Beyond an awareness of this reality (which should be helpful in and of itself), there are parenting implications. To move toward independence and a full life (a life of good choices, we all hope), teenagers need to exercise their "speculation muscle." They often won't go there on their own. But we can help. Set aside your agenda when your teenager starts asking (or implying) speculation questions, and engage him or her in the process. Don't just give the right answer (assuming you have one). Instead, do what Jesus did, and respond to a question with another question. Ask "what if" and "why" questions, which help your teenager exercise this new and critical ability.

Even my little example of Max and his strong, nameless emotion points to this. I would have done Max a great disservice if I had told him what he was feeling, or *told* him what he should be thinking.

Big Implication #2: Third-Person Perspective

Another enormous implication of abstract thinking is the ability to see things from a third-person perspective. In other words, to perceive yourself, or others, or a situation, from some other (or someone else's) point of view. In a sense, this is a version of speculation, since we usually don't *know* what that other perspective would be, and are only inferring or assuming.

An example will help us here:

Stand a 9-year-old girl in front of a mirror and ask her to describe herself. Her description will mostly consist of what she literally sees in front of her—physical characteristics that are concrete and indisputable. She might add some personality characteristics that she knows to be true of herself. The only external influence on her description, normally, will be what others have directly told her about herself.

Stand a 16-year-old girl in front of a mirror and ask her to describe herself, and you'll get a *very* different kind of answer. While she might still include a few concrete details, most of her description will be based on perception—who she sees herself to be, what she assumes others think of her, and (unfortunately) how she perceives she doesn't meet some cultural expectation.

Or:

Ask a 9-year-old son, after you've caught him lying to you, "How do you think this makes me feel?" He'll guess, based on your tone of voice and body language, that it makes you mad or sad. He might also guess based on his own experiences of being lied to. But any answer he provides is nothing more than a guess.

Ask a 16-year-old son, after you've caught him lying to you, "How do you think this makes me feel?" He doesn't have to guess (at least he has the brain capacity to respond with more than a guess). He can actually perceive how you would feel, or at least something close to it, based on his knowledge of you and your values, what he knows about your love for him or frustration with him, and a broader understanding of the complexities of raising a teenage son (of course, he'll still add your tone of voice and body language into the mix, as well as his own experiences).

Those markedly different responses capsulize this third-person thinking shift.

But this third-person perspective isn't only about self-perception. Thinking from other points of view helps us with a bunch of other complex adult functions. It can help us make better decisions, since we can remove ourselves and our own biases (to some extent) from the speculation process. It can help us engage and be present to people, when we have a sense of what they're feeling or experiencing. And it can cause us to reflect on big, complex questions about life and evil and goodness and culture and all of humanity.

One of the places I've often seen this play out is when I take teenagers on short-term mission trips. Due to the massive quantity and depth of the developmental changes occurring in their bodies and brains, teenagers are often rather narcissistic. They see themselves as the center of the universe (particularly younger teenagers). But when they encounter people with real needs, especially in a different cultural context, the experience can knock them off-balance, in a great way. They get a sense of themselves as part of a much larger story. They wonder why they have so much, while others have so little. They see, from outside of themselves, their own selfishness and materialism, and this messes with their priorities and values.

Other Implications

While the implications of abstract thinking we've talked about so far are the biggies, there's a host of additional ways this new ability reorients the lives of teenagers.

Empathy. Empathy and sympathy aren't really the same thing, of course. While you might think of empathy as a more intense version of sympathy, the real difference is connected to abstract thinking.

Empathy means you feel what the other person feels. Sympathy just means you feel what you feel, which is that you're sorry for the other person. Of course, we can't *actually* feel what another person feels, but abstract thought gives us the tools for truly sensing (not just guessing) what another is going through. Sympathy is an idea, but empathy is an experience.

(A quick reminder here: All of these abstract-thinking implications, including empathy, are new tools in the cognitive toolbox of teenagers. But that doesn't mean they have any idea how to use them, or will naturally utilize them each time a situation calls for them.)

Paradox. Just so we're all clear on this, a paradox is two statements (or a group of statements) that are both (or all) true, yet are in conflict with one another.

A common, iconic paradox is "Which came first, the chicken or the egg?"

Children are massively riddled with paradox. They just don't know it! So it would be completely normal for a 6-year-old to firmly believe two things that are in conflict with one another ("Shoes don't really make people faster" but "These shoes make me faster!"). Yet when confronted with a paradox, they'll tend to concretely pick a lane.

Abstract thinking, however, opens up the possibility for seemingly contradictory ideas to be held in tension with one another. For example, I can't tell you how many times I've had a middle schooler ask me, "Can God make a rock that's too heavy for him to lift?" Usually the middle schooler thinks he's about to trap me with his new brilliance. That's usually the point at which I start telling him about the great youth ministry at that other church down the road (I'm kidding).

But even the fact that this middle schooler would ask me the question, to which he knows there is no "correct" answer, shows his budding abstract thinking.

Paradox plays an enormous role in faith development. Don't get all bothered with me for this next illustration—I'm not trying to make any particular point other than one about paradox and faith: How can we truly love our neighbor more than ourselves, while still defending a military response to a global crisis? Again, I'm not trying to make a statement here; I'm merely suggesting that adult faith is *not* concrete and simplistic, but complex and full of paradox.

Everything else. I wrote in Chapter 1 that I think cognitive change is the biggest change your teenager is undergoing, with more profound impact on her life than the physical changes she's experiencing.

And here's why: In addition to the implications laid out in this chapter, the onset of abstract thought also plays out in a multitude of other teen-change areas. Abstract thinking is at the root of why your teenager often seems so emotional. It's the foundational element in why his friendships have changed over the past few years. It's the starting point for the separation you and your daughter are both experiencing as she moves toward independence. And it's the source code for your teenager moving toward a sustainable adult faith.

And that's what we're going to talk about in the next chapter!

CHAPTER 4: THE TRICKLE-DOWN EFFECT OF ABSTRACT THINKING (OR, WHY TEENAGERS ACT THE WAY THEY DO)

Ladies and Gentlemen, Moms and Dads, please buckle your safety belt low and tight across your lap, turn off all electronics (well, unless you're reading this on something electronic!), and prepare to say, "Wow, Marko, I had no idea my teenager's brain development explains that much about why he or she acts that way!"

Sorry, that was lame. Apparently I've been on too many planes recently. Read on.

Abstract Thinking and Emotions

Remember that happy-go-lucky preteen your teenager used to be? Remember when her emotions were fairly predictable? Remember when you could spot in a second the exact emotion your son was experiencing, because it was all over his face?

Now you have a teenager in your house whose emotions feel like a magic show—you know you're not seeing the whole story, but you have no idea what's actually going on. Why is your daughter so emotionally volatile? How is it that she can turn on a dime from carefree to furious, from distraught to "whatever"? And how is it that the "dime" is so apparently imperceptible (at least to adult eyes)?

If parents of teenagers see something of the developmental change taking place in their teenagers beyond the physical changes, emotional changes are the next-most obvious. You know I'm going to say it, so just say it with me: It's all because of their brains!

Emotions are abstract! So it makes sense that children and preteens would be limited in their experience of emotions, limited to understanding them in concrete terms.

I have found that the best metaphor for understanding this is to imagine that emotions are the colors on a painter's palette. A child has a small emotional palette, with the equivalent of primary colors, plus black and white. But at puberty, with the onset of abstract thinking, God swaps out that little limited palette with a new one: a large palette preloaded with dozens—if not hundreds—of emotional options and nuances.

But like a beginning painter, teenagers are not familiar with the colors on this palette, or the technique involved in blending them effectively. So they often paint their lives, emotionally, with one of two extremes:

- Bright, garish colors (emotions) that seem way too intense for the situation.

- A muddled, overblended version of beige.

(As an aside, when we combine their new abilities with cultural values, teenage girls often lean toward the bright and garish, while teenage boys often lean toward beige.)

I've often heard adults say that teenagers need to learn to control their emotions. But that's missing the point. Controlling them isn't much use if they don't understand them. So the task of adolescence, when it comes to emotions, is trying to learn—through trial and error—to understand this glorious diversity of emotions now at their disposal.

I see this change as one of the amazing, creative works of God. My favorite framing verse for understanding teenage emotions is John 10:10, where Jesus says these words:

"I have come that they may have life, and have it to the full."

In order for us to fully live, to wholly experience the life that God dreams for each of us, we are given the rich gift of complex and diverse emotion. And growing into an understanding of that experience is a sign of God's deep love for each of us, God's deep love for your son or daughter.

Abstract Thinking and Relationships

Here's my current best illustration of the relational change taking place in the lives and minds of teenagers:

Put a dozen 7-year-olds in a room with a big tub of Legos®, and you'll observe few problems. They'll play together or independently, but will mostly get along just fine. There might be a bully in the group who likes to smash other kids' structures, but the room will primarily be devoid of politics. The reason? Children aren't as differentiated from each other, and with a common focus (the Legos), they're concretely focused and oblivious to what it *means* that they're playing next to this kid or that kid.

Put a dozen 16-year-olds in a room (feel free to leave the Legos in there if you'd like!), and you'll have a *very* different scenario unfold. It's closely akin to the first episode of every season of the TV show *Survivor*, where everyone is immediately sizing each other up, looking for potential alliances, perceiving threats, and wondering if they'll be the first person voted off.

Certainly there are more than three, but the big three factors (all connected to abstract thinking) that bring change in adolescent friendship are:

- Individuation—the process of becoming one's own self, separated from parents and family. As a teenager begins to individuate, she becomes more aware of her own uniquenesses, interests, values, and preferences. And those have friendship implications.

- Affinity—one of the big three adolescent tasks (the other two being identity and autonomy). Affinity asks the question, "To whom and where do I belong?" This new, abstract question pushes teenagers to look for friends with whom they share a common interest, rather than merely the friend who's close by (childhood friendships are usually born out of proximity).

- Third-person perspective—one of our "biggies" from the last chapter. This ability to perceive oneself from another's point of view causes teenagers to not only consider how a friend (or potential friend) might perceive them, but also causes them to consider how others will perceive them *based* on their friendships.

Abstract Thinking and Independence

While your son or daughter always had his or her own unique interests and personality, apart from yours, children usually bear a strong resemblance to their parents in terms of values, opinions, and beliefs. It's rare I find a sixth-grader who, during an election period when they're mildly aware of national politics, would claim to have a political affinity to "the other party" from their parents.

But abstract thinking, and that process of individuation I just mentioned, expedites the process of independence. When you feel tension with your son, or when your daughter espouses a viewpoint or belief that differs from your own, they're showing you their brains. And that process is not only normal, it's healthy and necessary (though it doesn't always feel good, and doesn't always come out in nice ways!).

Remember: Your goal as a parent is that your teenager would become independent. Not that he won't still need you or need other people—we're made for community and complementing one another. But you *want* your teenager (I hope, if your parenting values are good) to move to a place of autonomy by the time he finishes his teenage years.

If this all feels overwhelming to you, go back and read the section on Boundaries and Freedom in Chapter 2.

Abstract Thinking and Faith

See if you can pick the concrete, nonabstract idea out of this list:

- The Bible is God's revelation to us about himself, ourselves, and all of creation.

- Jesus saves us.

- God's essence is love.

- Following Jesus is what discipleship is all about.

- God has always existed and is eternal in all ways.

- God the Father, Jesus, and the Holy Spirit are one.

- Jesus became a man without giving up being God.

- God desires that we live selfless lives, serving others.

I could easily make the list 10 times as long, but let's stop there. The answer to my question about which of those is concrete and nonabstract: none of them. They're all abstract. In fact, pretty much everything to do with faith is abstract.

And while Jesus encourages us to have childlike faith, he certainly doesn't encourage us to have *childish* faith. So if your teenager is going to have a sustainable faith that last beyond Sunday school and bedtime prayers (good things!), she's going to have to seriously employ her abstract-thinking muscle!

Recently, I was having a conversation with the leaders of a youth ministry organization called Barefoot Ministries (they're the youth ministry resource arm of the Nazarene Publishing House). And they shared a progression of faith I found extremely helpful:

Simplicity ➡ Complexity ➡ Perplexity ➡ Humility

The idea is that new Christians, whether children or adults, usually have a beautiful simplicity to their faith. "God loves me and Jesus saved me and nothing else matters." But at some point in our spiritual journeys (this happens during adolescence for those raised in faith, thanks to abstract thinking), we begin to realize that aspects of our belief are more complex. Eventually, we get to a point where there are at least *some* things that are truly perplexing (paradox!). If we hold on to faith through those times, we can move into a space of humility where we choose to exercise faith, knowing we don't have all the answers.

The rub is this: When Christian teenagers start to experience complexity and perplexity in their faith, we (parents and the church) often freak out. It *looks* like they might be *losing* their faith! We push them back, longing for them to return to that beautiful place of simplicity.

But unless we allow them the space to move into and through complexity and perplexity (this isn't abandonment, by the way, but should be an active engagement and co-journeying), we stunt their faith development and reduce the likelihood that they'll have an active faith as adults.

Whew. Parenting teenagers is hard!

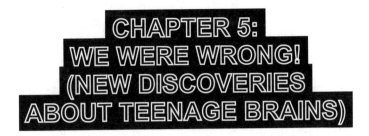

CHAPTER 5: WE WERE WRONG! (NEW DISCOVERIES ABOUT TEENAGE BRAINS)

Before we wrap up this pint-sized book, there's some breaking news. Well, at least it's breaking news in the scope of what the medical world has known about teenage brains, in that it's a set of brand-new discoveries in the past 15 years or so. And this new stuff is far from merely academic—it offers tons of explanations into teenage behaviors, as well as some pointed challenges about parenting a teenage brain.

The surprising truth is that, until the last decade, we've known very little about teenage brains (and children's brains, for that matter). Most of what we thought we knew was observed through behavior, was assumed, or was based on X-rays and knowledge of adult brains. That's because it was considered unethical to open up the skulls of children and teenagers and study healthy, live brains (fair enough)!

But with the invention and acceptance of the MRI, real-time noninvasive study of healthy brains became possible.

For hundreds of years, the entire medical and scientific community held to the assumption that brains were fully formed, on average, by 6 years old. After that, the brain grew in size a bit, and certainly grew in speed and functionality. But the assumption was that "it was all there."

The biggest shock (really, this was a shock to the scientific community) was the finding that brains are not fully formed until somewhere around 25 years old. Prior to that, there are important parts of the brain that are, literally, physically underdeveloped.

That's kind of a big deal!

Big Discovery #1: Meet the Temporal Lobes

Human brains are usually talked about in terms of having four lobes (sections), mirrored on both the left and right sides of the brain (so, I suppose it's actually eight lobes!). While various brain functions aren't completely isolated to one or another lobe, there do seem to be particular functions that take place primarily in one lobe. For instance, the occipital lobes at the back of your head are responsible for all things vision-related.

The temporal lobes are an area of significant underdevelopment in teenage brains. The temporal lobes—we each have a left one and a right one—are responsible, among other things, for emotional interpretation and understanding. They're underdeveloped in all teenagers, but are significantly more underdeveloped in guys (yeah, moms, we know you're laughing right now; cut it out).

It's important to think through how we respond to this information. One response would be to say, "Well, I guess teenagers are just not capable of emotional understanding, so I should stop expecting it or hoping for it." That, my parent friends, would be lame (though not uncommon). The research does *not* prove that teenagers are incapable. In fact, there's research to show that teenage brains compensate in other ways for this limitation.

So I believe the healthy response for parents (and youth workers, for that matter) is a combination of patience and understanding, coupled with a tour-guide approach to helping teenagers interpret their emotions and the emotions of others.

When Max, my 14-year-old son, completely misreads the sad emotion on my wife's face and in her voice, I neither ignore it and assume he's incapable, nor come down on him for his ridiculous misjudgment of reality. Instead, I come alongside him, helping him to see what's really going on, helping him to *exercise* that brain function.

Big Discovery #2: Meet the Source of Your Parental Frustration, the Frontal Lobe

The biggest news in all this new brain discovery stuff, and the aspect that's been reported the most often in more popular media, is the underdevelopment of the prefrontal cortex in teenagers (part of what's more commonly called the frontal lobe, or frontal lobes). In fact, this new information (and, I believe, the incorrect application of it) has been so broadly written about that I've seen it pop up in everything from young adult fiction to auto insurance ads ("Why do teenagers drive like they're missing a piece of their brain? Because they are.").

The frontal lobe is often called the brain's CEO, or the decision-making center. Here's a partial list of the functions it's responsible for:

- Decision-making

- Wisdom

- Prioritization

- Impulse control

- Planning

- Organization

- Focus

If you made a list of those words' opposites (such as unfocused, disorganized, lacking wisdom, and absence of impulse control), you'd have a fairly good working definition of how most people view teenagers! And what we've come to learn is that there's a physiological reason for this.

But the conclusions being disseminated about this discovery have become a bit of a pet peeve for me. Hear this: There is *no* research that shows a *causal* relationship between these underdeveloped areas of teenage brains and behavior. In other words, just because a particular segment of the brain is still growing does *not* mean that teenagers are incapable of making good decisions or exercising wisdom (or any of the rest of that list). Those sorts of unfair (and illogical) conclusions really amount to negative prejudicial stereotypes based on a physical characteristic.

We did the same thing with women for centuries: We said that, since women have smaller brains, on average, than men, they are clearly not capable of higher thought, voting rights, and even intelligent discourse. We (as humans) went down the same road by assigning negative stereotypes to Jews and people of African descent, and reverse-engineered our prejudices onto physical characteristics.

I think the same thing is happening to teenagers *right now*. We're taking our already-negative perceptions of teenagers and reverse-applying it to these new brain findings. And I refuse to accept that. As a parent of a teenager, I hope you'll stand with me on this one.

We also don't have any idea if the underdevelopment of frontal lobes on teenagers has always been that way (which seems to be the uncritical assumption on the part of many) or is the result of a culture that doesn't expect teenagers to use that part of their brains (Robert Epstein, referenced earlier, would argue strongly for the latter).

That doesn't mean I'm ignoring the underdevelopment of frontal lobes in teenagers! No way! I'm fascinated by this discovery, and I am rearranging my youth ministry and parenting approaches in light of it. But that primarily means extra doses of patience and understanding, and a desire to help teenagers exercise those parts of their brains.

Remember, as I've said at various points in this book: How can we expect our sons and daughters to actually *be* responsible if we never give them the opportunity to try it out (and fail)? How can we expect them to use their God-given brains if we don't allow those brains to mature?

Big Discovery #3: Rerouting the Highways (or, Neurons Grow Then Go)

A final new discovery about teenage brains has really captured my imagination and impacted my parenting.

Neurons are the "electrical wiring" of the brain and, when grouped together, are referred to as neural pathways. These neural pathways are the information superhighways of the brain and the means by which information moves around. By the way, best estimates of normal neuron counts in a human brain are *between 80 billion and 120 billion*. That's a lot of neurons!

The new discovery is this: A couple of years prior to the onset of puberty, the brain goes into a massive growth frenzy, adding millions of additional neurons. Then, at puberty, a switch is tripped, and the process reverses itself. Over the two to four years following the onset of puberty (roughly 11 or 12 through 15 or 16), the brain cuts back millions of neurons.

But that proliferation and winnowing isn't the most interesting part. The most interesting part is the selection process for neuron elimination. Jay Giedd, the lead researcher on teenage brains at the National Institutes of Health, calls it a "use it or lose it principle."[3] In other words, those neurons (and neural pathways) that are used during the young and middle teen years get to stay and play—and those that aren't used go bye-bye.

Giedd even goes on to say (these are some amazing words you're about to read) that the brain is "hard-wired" during the teen years for how it will function throughout adulthood.

In other words: If a teenager spends a massive quantity of time playing video games, she'll hard-wire her brain for the thought processes utilized in that pursuit (by that way, that's not *all* bad, and could result in quick choice-making and problem-solving, among other things). If a teenager engages in arts during the teen years, he will lock in artistic brain processes that will become a part of his way of thinking for life. If a teenager is forced to memorize giant quantities of information—well, you get the picture.

This isn't to say that the brain can't learn new things, or even new ways of thinking, in adulthood. But it is saying that certain ways of thinking are *tuned* during the teen years, and that's a tuning that sticks.

As a parent, this boils down to stewardship. The question that has brought about a shift in my own parenting since I've learned this reality: How can I best *steward* the opportunity I have to permanently shape my teenagers' brains? And more specifically, how can I best steward the opportunity I have to shape their brains for a lifetime of robust faith?

A final thought (not about neurons): You are the indisputably biggest influence in the life of your teenager. While you might be led to believe this isn't true, and that peers or culture have a bigger influence, research has shown over and over again that parents are the biggest influence in the lives of teenagers. One extremely credible researcher (Christian Smith, in response to his National Study of Youth and Religion) says that the best indicator of a teenager's faith is the faith of his or her parents. [4]

My hope and prayer is that you've gained some understanding about what's going on inside your teenager's head, why she acts *that* way, and what a fantastic opportunity you have to come alongside your teenager in helping him reach adulthood.

Parenting teenagers is tough work, to be sure. But it's also one of the greatest privileges we'll ever have. Now, go shape that brain!

ENDNOTES

1. Robert Epstein, *Teen 2.0* (Fresno, CA: Quill Driver Books, 2010), 3.

2. Michael Chabon, *Manhood for Amateurs: The Pleasures and Regrets of a Husband, Father, and Son* (New York, NY: Harper, 2009), 65-66.

3. pbs.org/wgbh/pages/frontline/shows/teenbrain/interviews/giedd.html

4. youthandreligion.org

Check out all the books in our
PARENT'S GUIDE Series!